Make Your Own
GREETING CARDS

Steve & Megumi Biddle

Dover Publications, Inc.
Mineola, New York

ABOUT THE AUTHORS

Steve Biddle is a professional entertainer and origami expert. He has been teaching origami to children and adults since 1976. While he was in Japan studying under the top Japanese Origami Masters, he met and married his wife Megumi. Megumi is one of the foremost Japanese paper-artists working in *Washi,* hand-made Japanese paper, and her work has received many top awards in Japan and abroad. She has designed for some of Japan's top fashion designers, and has worked on many award-winning commercials for Japanese television. Since their return to England, Steve and Megumi have taken their craft all over the country to schools, festivals, and arts centers, and have designed for television and feature films. They present origami as entertainment, art, and education to young and old alike.

PUBLISHER'S NOTE

The eight sheets of cardstock provided at the back of the book will help to get you started making your own greeting cards. The supplied cardstock is slightly smaller than the recommended size, so you may need to adjust your measurements accordingly in order to complete some of the projects. You can purchase additional cardstock at your local crafts store or through online sources.

Copyright

Copyright © 1992, 2013 by Steven and Megumi Biddle
All rights reserved.

Bibliographical Note

This Dover edition, first published in 2013, is a slightly altered republication of the work originally published by Red Fox, a division of Random House, Ltd., in 1992. Sixteen sheets of blank cardstock have been added for this edition.

Library of Congress Cataloging-in-Publication Data

Biddle, Steve.
　　Make your own greeting cards / Steve & Megumi Biddle.
　　　　pages cm.
　　"Originally published by Red Fox, a division of Random House, Ltd., in 1992"—Title page verso.
　　　ISBN-13: 978-0-486-49161-5
　　　ISBN-10: 0-486-49161-7
　　　1. Greeting cards—Design. 2. Paper work. I. Biddle, Megumi. II. Title.
TT872.B53 2013
745.594'1—dc23

2013015449

Manufactured in the United States by Courier Corporation
49161701　　2013
www.doverpublications.com

INTRODUCTION

Only a little imagination and a few simple techniques are required to design a greeting card. This is what MAKE YOUR OWN GREETING CARDS is all about.

As craft paper and card are some of the cheapest materials available, many of the projects in this book can be started with the minimum of outlay. Each project introduces a new design or technique, so that by the time you have worked through the book, you will have learned many of the skills involved in making greeting cards.

Before you choose which card to make, we suggest that you read General Materials and Techniques and Greeting Card Sizes, as these sections cover many of the materials, tools and techniques needed.

The papers mentioned by name are recommended from personal experience. There are, however, many other, equally effective, papers available (which may differ by trade name). Also we have found materials required for making greeting cards in the most unlikely places, ranging from newsstands to fashion shops. So be persistent and search around carefully.

To help you become accomplished in making greetings cards, here are some very useful tips:

- *Work on a flat surface.*
- *Make your folds and cuts neat and accurate.*
- *Press your folds into place by running your thumb nail along them.*
- *Try to take great care in obtaining the right kind of paper that will be ideal for the card that you plan to make. More often than not, this will help to enhance the finished product.*
- *Above all, if nothing works, just place your card to one side and come back to it another day with a fresh mind.*

In making greeting cards it is the finishing touches and personal style that will make your designs look professional. By all means aim to copy the cards exactly as they appear in the photographs at first but what is important is your own personal touch and how you develop the illustrated ideas.

We hope that you have a great deal of fun and enjoyment with MAKE YOUR OWN GREETING CARDS.

Steve and Megumi

ACKNOWLEDGEMENTS

We would like to thank Mitsuhiro Matsumoto, Sue Rogers and Nicole van Spronsen for sending us such original and beautiful greeting cards. Also our deepest thanks go to John Cunliffe for his help and support.

CONTENTS

GENERAL MATERIALS AND TECHNIQUES

Before you start it is recommended that you read this section, and the section on page 6, thoroughly. They describe the many materials, techniques and skills that recur in the instructions.

and writing messages and a few other everyday materials that can be found around the home, or bought from any good stationery shop for just a few dollars.

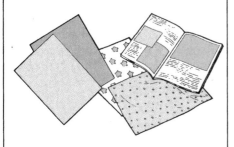

PAPER
To make the cards in this book you will need craft paper/card and wrapping paper in a variety of colors. These types of materials can be obtained from art and craft stores and stationery stores. An 8½ x 11 in. sheet of craft paper makes a gift card of reasonable size.

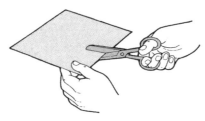

SCISSORS
Remember to use scissors carefully as they can be very sharp. For a sharp, clean cut always keep the blades at 90 degrees to the paper and do not twist and turn them around.

USING A CRAFT KNIFE
Remember that a craft knife can be very sharp. So when using one, always tell an adult what you are going to do (or ask them to help you), and always do any cutting or scoring on a piece of old board, so that you do not cut yourself or damage any surfaces.

SCORING
The most common technique in card making is the score, which lets your material be folded in clean, sharp lines.

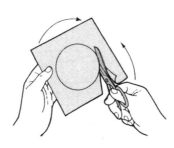

TOOLS
More often than not all that you require for card making is a tube of stick glue, a compass, craft or cutting knife, scissors, ruler (metal or with a metal edge), pencil and lots of old newspaper to cover your work space. You will also need felt-tip pens for coloring in designs

CUTTING
A solid line means "cut the paper." The solid line shows the position of the cut. When cutting a circle or curved line, always cut around the pencil outline by turning your material as you go along, rather than the scissors. This will help to prevent any sharp corners in the finished shape.

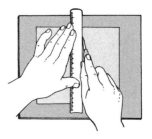

1   Place a metal ruler next to the line to be folded and hold it down firmly, as shown. Then carefully guide the point of a craft knife . . .

Card-making materials

2 along the ruler's metal edge, so cutting through about half the thickness of your material. Be careful not to cut all the way through.

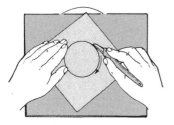

3 Circles and curved lines can be scored freehand, along a round object such as a saucer or a tin can. For smoother lines try moving the paper and holding the craft knife still.

4 Your material is always folded away from the scored line. Sometimes you can score your material by using a ruler, spatula or the pointed end of a compass.

HANDLING OF TOOLS

Always take great care when handling any sharp edged or pointed tools, as not to cut yourself. It is a good idea to keep them in a safe place, like a box with a lid, and out of reach of any younger members of the family.

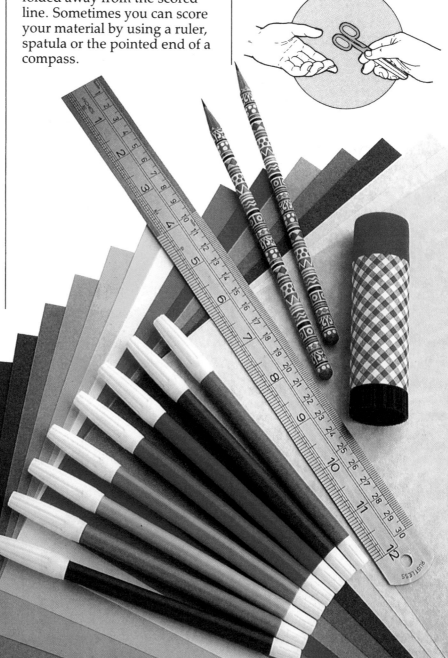

GREETING CARD SIZES

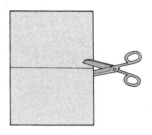

To make many of the projects found in Make Your Own Greeting Cards *you will need a double card, and for a few others a single card. Here are quick and easy ways to make them.*

You will need: *For each card an 8½ x 11 in. sheet of craft paper Scissors*

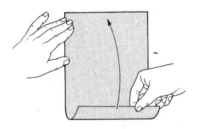

1 DOUBLE CARD: Place the rectangle of craft paper lengthways on, and hold down the top edge. Lift the bottom edge up . . .

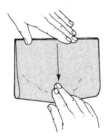

2 and bring it up to meet the top edge. Keeping the edges together, run your forefinger down the middle of the paper to the bottom edge, to fix the middle of the fold.

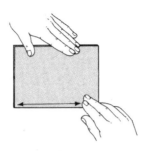

3 Run your forefinger along the bottom edge to both sides, so pressing the fold in place.

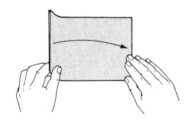

4 Fold the paper in half from left to right.

5 Press the fold in place, . . .

6 thereby completing the double card.

7 SINGLE CARD: Begin with a completed step 3. Open out the paper completely. Cut along the middle fold-line, so making two rectangles. Put one rectangle aside and with the other . . .

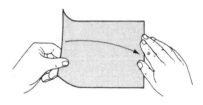

8 repeat step 4.

9 Repeat step 5 . . .

10 thereby completing the single card.

ENVELOPES

Here are three quick and easy ways for making an envelope to match a greeting card. To send your envelope through the mail, do not forget to address it and to stick on a stamp.

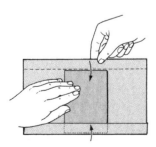

You will need: *For each envelope an 8½ x 11 in. sheet of craft paper*
A greeting card
Scissors
Glue

FANCY ENVELOPE

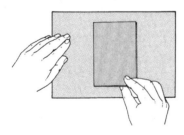

1   Place the rectangle of craft paper sideways on. Turn the greeting card lengthways on, and place it centrally on to the paper.

2   Fold the top and bottom edges over the card.

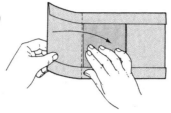

3   Fold the left-hand side over the card.

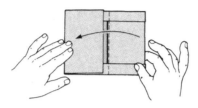

4   Fold the right-hand side over the card.

5   Press the paper flat.

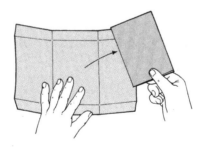

6   Open out the paper completely, and put the card aside.

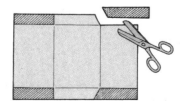

7   Carefully cut away and discard the shaded parts, as shown, so making a top and bottom tab.

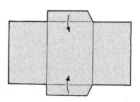

8   Fold the tabs over along the existing fold-lines.

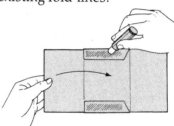

9   Apply glue to the tabs. Do not apply glue near their sloping edges. Fold the left-hand side over along the existing fold-line and on to the glued tabs. Press firmly.

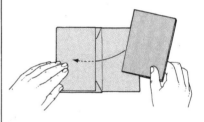

10   When the glue is dry, insert the card inside, by going between the front and back layers of paper.

11   On the right-hand section of paper cut away and discard the shaded parts, as shown, so making a decorative flap.

12   Fold the flap over along the existing fold-line. Glue it down, thereby completing the fancy envelope.

GEOMETRIC ENVELOPE

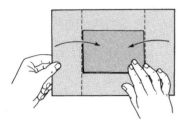

1 Place the rectangle of craft paper sideways on. Turn the greeting card sideways on, and place it centrally on to the paper. Fold the sides over the card.

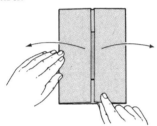

2 Press the sides flat and unfold them.

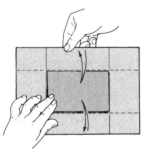

3 Fold the top and bottom edges over the card. Press the edges flat and unfold them.

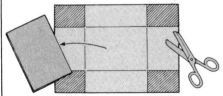

4 Put the card aside. Cut away and discard the shaded parts, as shown, so making four tabs.

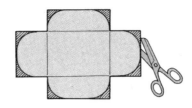

5 Cut away and discard the shaded parts, as shown.

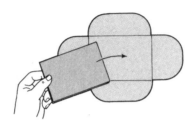

6 Replace the card, centrally on to the paper.

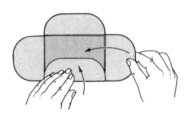

7 Fold the bottom and right-hand tab over along the existing fold-lines.

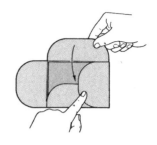

8 Fold the top tab over along the existing fold-line.

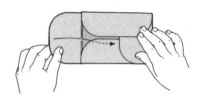

9 Repeat step 8 with the left-hand tab, but at the same time slide its lower half underneath the bottom tab.

10 Press the tabs down firmly, thereby completing the geometric envelope.

ORIGAMI ENVELOPE

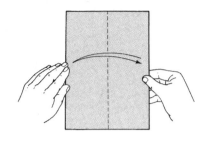

1 Place the rectangle of craft paper lengthways on. Fold it in half from side to side. Press the paper flat and unfold it.

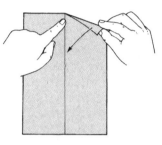

2 Fold the top right-hand corner over to meet the middle fold-line.

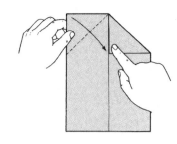

3 Repeat step 2 with the top left-hand corner, so making a shape that looks like the roof of a house.

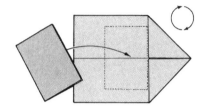

4 Turn the roof around, so that it points to the right. Turn the greeting card lengthways on, and place it centrally on to the paper, adjacent to the roof.

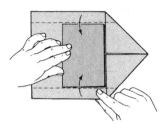

5 Fold the top and bottom edges over the card.

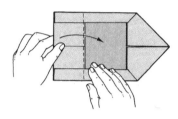

6 Fold the left-hand side over the card.

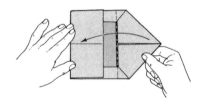

7 Fold the right-hand point over the card.

8 Glue the point down and add a little fancy decoration, thereby completing the origami envelope.

From the left: Fancy envelope; Geometric envelope; Origami envelope

RIBBON DECORATIONS

These decorations will give a professional look to any greeting card. They are very easy to make if you follow the illustrations carefully.

You will need: *Ribbon*
Scissors
Sticky tape
A greeting card

1 BOW: Unwind a little of the ribbon from its spool. With the free end of the ribbon make a fair-sized loop. Try to make the protruding . . .

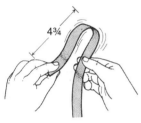

2 "tail" longer than the actual loop. From its spool unwind a little more ribbon and bring it up, over and...

3 behind the loop you are holding, so creating a band of ribbon.

4 Unwind a little more ribbon and push it underneath the band of ribbon, as shown, so making . . .

5 another equal-sized loop.

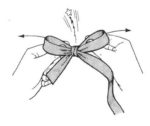

6 Hold the loops by their lower layers and pull them apart, so tightening the band of ribbon.

7 Finally, cut the ribbon free from its spool, so making another "tail" which is the same length as the previous one.

8 CURLS: Cut a 4¾ in. length of ribbon.

9 Using a small piece of sticky tape, fasten one end of the ribbon on to the card in an appropriate place.

10 Cut several slits in the ribbon's free end.

11 Carefully pull the ribbon into strips, starting from the free end and . . .

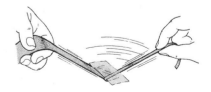

12 continuing as far as the sticky tape.

13 Holding the sticky tape down firmly, place one strip of ribbon between your thumb and the CLOSED blades of the scissors. Draw the blades firmly across the ribbon, so . . .

14 curling it in the process. The strength of the finished curl depends upon how firmly the closed blades are drawn across the ribbon. Finally, curl the remaining strips.

15 Try to make the bow and curls out of a gift ribbon matching the color of the finished greeting card.

PECKING CHICK

This delightful action design makes an ideal place card for a party.

You will need: *Compass*
Pencil
Ruler
An 8½ x 11 in. sheet of yellow craft paper
Scissors
Stick glue
Felt-tip pen

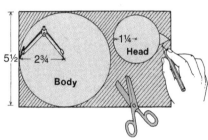

1 Using the compass, pencil and ruler, mark and measure out this chick design on to the rectangle of yellow craft paper, as shown. Carefully cut along your pencil lines. Do not discard any excess paper.

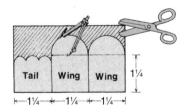

2 Using the compass, pencil and ruler, mark and measure out the chick's tail and wings on to the excess paper, as shown. Carefully cut around your pencil lines and discard the shaded part.

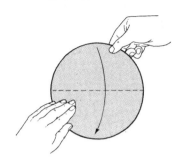

3 Fold the body circle in half from top to bottom.

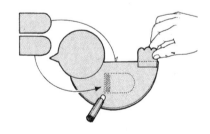

4 Glue the chick's head on to its body, as shown by the shaded part.

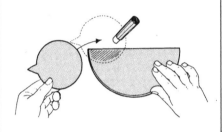

5 Glue the chick's wings on to either side of its body, as shown by the shaded part. Glue the tail on to the body.

11

6 Using the felt-tip pen, draw on the chick's eyes. Fold the wings slightly away from the body. When you tap the chick's tail, it pecks for food.

7 Finally, write a message inside the card.

GOOD LUCK

Try to keep the paper in the same place on the table during the folding of this card. This will help you when you are making the spring.

You will *Scissors*
need: *An 8½ x 11 in. sheet of black craft paper*
Ruler
Felt-tip pen
Stick glue
Compass
Pencil
Penny
Small piece of green paper
A single card

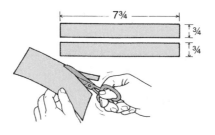

1 Cut two strips of black craft paper measuring ¾ x 7¾ in. Using the felt-tip pen, label one strip **A** and the other **B**.

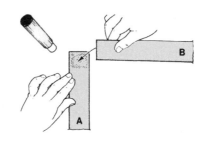

2 Apply glue at the end of strip A. Lay strip B at right angles to strip A on to the glued area. Allow the glue to dry.

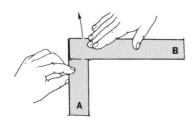

3 Fold strip A up over strip B.

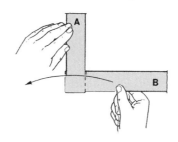

4 Fold strip B, across to the left, over strip A.

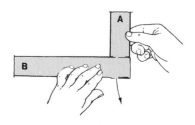

5 Fold strip A down over strip B.

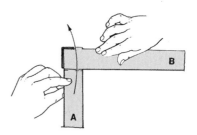

6 Fold strip B, across to the right, over strip A.

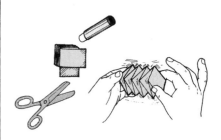

7 Repeat step 3.

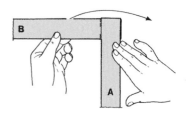

8 Continue overlapping the strips until all of the paper is folded. Apply glue under the top flap of paper and press firmly. Cut off any excess paper, so making a folded spring. Pull the spring out slightly.
(turn to page 14)

From the top: Good luck; Pop-up penguin; Pecking chick

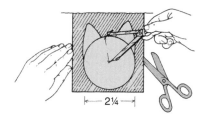

9 Using the compass, pencil and ruler, mark and measure out a cat's face on the black craft paper as shown. Carefully cut around your pencil lines and discard the shaded part.

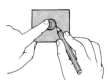

10 Using the pencil, mark around the penny on to the small piece of green paper. Carefully cut around your pencil line and discard the excess paper.

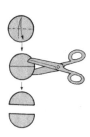

11 Fold the green circle in half from bottom to top. Press the circle flat and unfold it. Cut along the middle fold-line, so making two semicircles. These are the cat's eyes.

12 Glue the eyes on to the cat's face, as shown.

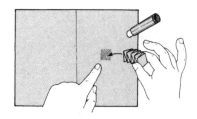

13 Apply a little glue on to the middle of the right-hand half of the card. Press one end of the spring on to the glue.

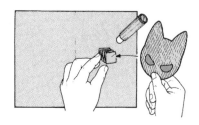

14 Apply glue on to the other end of the spring and attach it to the back of the cat's face.

15 The cat's face will stand out and . . .

16 wobble about when the card is opened. Finally, decorate the front of the card and write a message inside.

POP-UP PENGUIN

Do try to fold this design accurately. Otherwise the finished greeting card will not look neat and tidy.

You will need: *Scissors*
An 8½ x 11 in. sheet of craft paper, navy blue on one side and white on the other
Ruler
Pencil
Stick glue
A single card

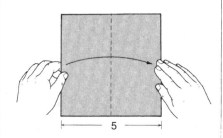

1 From the rectangle of navy blue craft paper, cut a square of paper measuring 5 x 5 in. Fold it in half from left to right, with the colored side on top.

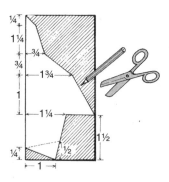

2 Using the pencil and ruler, mark and measure out this penguin design on to the square, from the folded side, as shown. Carefully cut around your pencil lines and discard the shaded parts.

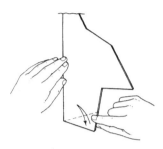

3 Fold the bottom points over, as shown by the dotted lines in step 2. Press the points flat and unfold them.

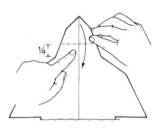

4 Open out the paper completely. Fold the top point over, as far as shown, with the white side on top.

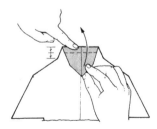

5 Fold the top point back over, as far as shown, so . . .

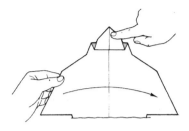

6 making a small pleat. Fold the paper in half from left to right.

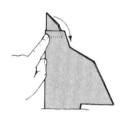

7 Pull the top point down, so . . .

8 that it sticks out from the folded side. Press the paper flat, thereby slightly rearranging the inside layers of paper.

9 Fold the topmost layer of paper over, as shown by the dotted lines. Repeat this step behind. Fold the bottom points behind along the fold-lines made in step 3, so making two tabs.

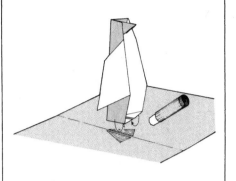

10 Open out the single card completely. Open out the penguin slightly. Apply glue on to the base of the tabs and attach them on either side of the card's middle fold-line, as shown by the shaded parts.

11 Close the card with the penguin inside and press firmly. Open the card. The penguin will pop-up. Finally, decorate the front of the card and write a message inside.

POP-UP RABBITS

This design would make the perfect birthday card for a younger brother or sister.

You will need:
Scissors
Ruler
Two 8½ x 11 in. sheets of craft paper, one white and the other green
Compass
Pencil
Felt-tip pen
A single card
Stick glue

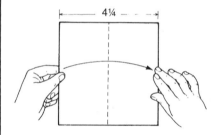

1   Cut a 4¼ in. square from the white craft paper. Fold it in half from left to right.

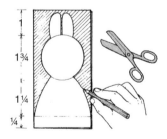

2   Using the compass, pencil and ruler, mark and measure out this rabbit design on paper, as shown. Carefully cut around your pencil line and discard the shaded part. Open up the design to make…

3   two rabbits, which are joined together. Using the felt-tip pen, draw on facial details, paws, carrot and a bow tie. Fold the bottom edge over along the ¼ in. pencil line marked in step 2. Press the edge flat and unfold it, so making a tab.

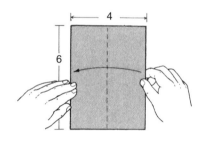

4   Cut a 4 x 6 in. rectangle of green craft paper. Fold it in half from right to left.

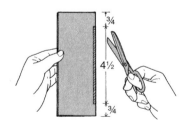

5   From the folded side, cut a slot in the paper that is 4½ in. long and is a distance of ¾ in. from the top and bottom edges. Discard the shaded part.

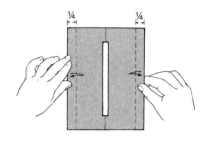

6   Open the paper completely. Fold over ¼ in. from either side. Press the sides flat and unfold them, making two tabs. This is the rabbits' burrow.

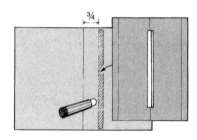

7   Open out the single card completely. Apply glue on to the back of the burrow's left hand tab and attach it to the right hand half of the card, at a point that is ¾ in. from the middle fold line.

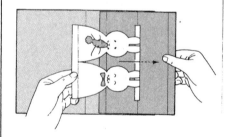

8   Turn the rabbits sideways on, and push their ears through the burrow's slot.

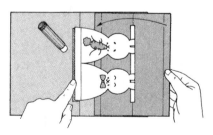

9   Apply glue on to the back of the rabbit's tab and attach it on to the card, as shown by the shaded part. Make sure that the tab's fold-line is positioned on top of the card's middle fold-line. Fold the burrow in half from right to left.

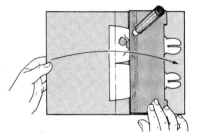

10   Apply glue on to the burrow's top tab, as shown by the shaded part. Close the card in half from left to right and . . .

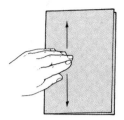

11   press firmly.

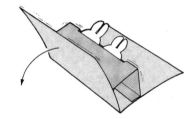

12   Make sure that the card opens and closes easily.

13   By opening and closing the card the rabbits will pop-up and down. Finally, decorate the front of the card and write a message inside.

Pop-up rabbits

17

THREE-DIMENSIONAL CARD

The following design shows you how to create a simple three-dimensional effect that will pop-up when the card is opened.

You will need: *A double card*
Scissors
Compass
Ruler
Felt-tip pen
Piece of craft paper the same color as the double card
Stick glue

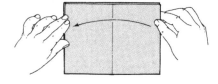

1 Turn the double card around so that the folded edge is at the bottom. Open it out from right to left.

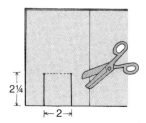

2 Along the left-hand half of the folded edge make two vertical cuts, as shown, so making an inside section.

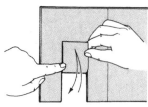

3 Fold the inside section over as far as it will go. Press the section flat and unfold it.

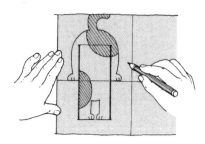

4 Open out the card completely, from top to bottom. Using the felt-tip pen, fill the space between and around the vertical cuts with the body of a dog. Place the dog's back legs on to the horizontal middle fold-line and its front legs adjacent to the bottom of the vertical cuts, as shown.

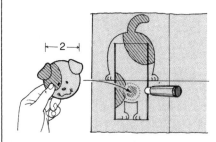

5 Using the compass, ruler and felt-tip pen, mark and measure out and color in the dog's face (see page 20) on to the craft paper, as shown. Carefully cut around your pen lines and discard any excess paper. Glue the face on to the body, as shown by the shaded part.

6 Fold the right-hand side behind to the left-hand side.

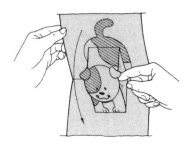

7 Close the card in half from top to bottom, while at the same time gently pulling the dog towards you. Press firmly.

8 Open the card. The dog will pop-up. Finally, decorate the front of the card and write a message inside. Why not design some three-dimensional cards of your own?

EASTER CARD

This design has several supports to which cut out shapes can be glued. It is an ideal way of creating three-dimensional versions of box-like subjects such as a house or a nesting hen.

You will need: *An 8½ x 11 in. sheet of yellow craft paper*
Scissors
Ruler
Pencil
Felt-tip pen
A single card
Stick glue

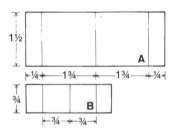

1 Cut two rectangles of yellow craft paper, one measuring 1½ x 4 in. and the other ¾ x 2¼ in. Using the pencil and ruler, mark and measure them out, as shown.

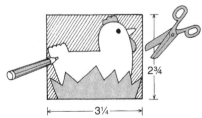

2 Cut a rectangle of craft paper measuring 2¾ x 3¼ in. Using the felt tip pen, draw this nesting hen design on to the rectangle, as shown. Carefully cut around your pen lines and discard any excess paper. Glue the face on to the body, as shown by the shaded part.

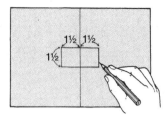

3 Open out the single card completely. Around the card's middle fold-line and an equal distance from the top and bottom edges, mark and measure out a 1½ x 3 in. rectangle, as shown.

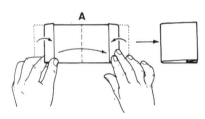

4 Fold rectangle A's side over along the ¼ in. pencil lines (see step 1), so making two tabs. Now fold rectangle A in half from left to right and press firmly.

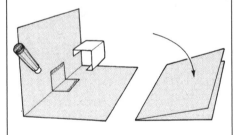

5 Open rectangle A into a half cube. Apply glue on to the base of the tabs and attach them on to the card, as shown. Make sure that the card closes and opens easily.

6 Glue the nesting hen on to one side of the half cube, making sure that the bottom of the design is no lower than the bottom of the cube. When the card closes, the hen should be completely inside the card.

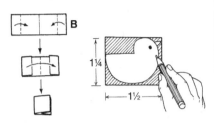

7 Repeat step 4 with rectangle B. Cut a rectangle of yellow craft paper measuring 1¼ x 1½ in. Using the felt-tip pen, draw this chick design on to the rectangle as shown. Carefully cut around your pen lines and discard the shaded parts.

8 Repeat steps 5 and 6 with rectangle B and the chick. Close the card with the designs inside and press firmly.

9 Open the card. The nesting hen and chick will stand up. Finally, decorate the front of the card and write a message inside.

From left to right: Three-dimensional card; Pop-up bird; Easter card

POP-UP BIRD

When this card is opened, part of the design pops right out above the rest of the card. With some slight variations in the folding and cutting you can develop some original ideas.

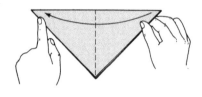

You will need: *An 8½ x 11 in. sheet of craft paper*
Scissors
Pencil
An envelope (see page 7)
Felt-tip pen

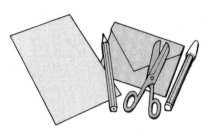

1 Place the rectangle of craft paper sideways on. Fold the left-hand side over to lie along the top edge, so making a triangle.

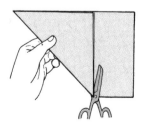

2 Cut along the right-hand side edge of the triangle.

3 Turn the triangle around so that the tip points towards you. Place the rectangle aside.

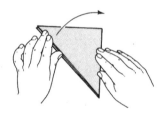

4 Fold the triangle in half from right to left.

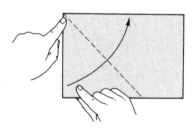

5 Lift the top half up along the middle fold-line.

6 Start to open the paper out . . .

7 and press it down neatly . . .

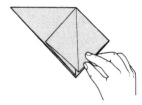

8 into a diamond. Press the paper flat.

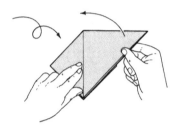

9 Turn the paper over from side to side. Repeat steps 5 to 8, so making . . .

10 the traditional origami preliminary base. Press the base flat.

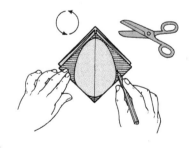

11 Turn the base around, so the open layers are pointing away from you. Using the pencil, mark out this egg shape on to the base, as shown. Carefully cut around your pencil lines and discard the shaded parts.

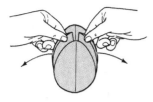

12 Open out the paper completely. Do 'NOT' press it flat.

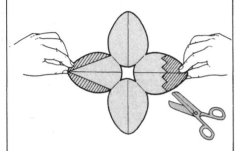

13 Cut out the bird's neck and tail as shown. Discard the shaded parts.

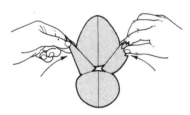

14 Carefully re-fold the paper back to the egg shape.

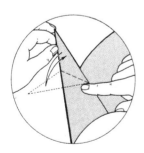

15 Separate slightly the front and back layers of paper, so that you can see the inside left-hand point. Fold the point over, into the position as shown by the dotted lines. Press the point flat and unfold it.

16 Now inside reverse fold the point. This is what you do, place your thumb into the point's groove, and . . .

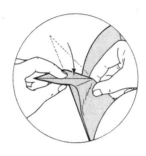

17 with your forefinger on top, pull the point down . . .

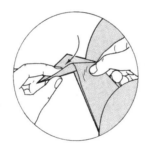

18 inside itself, along the fold-lines made in step 15.

19 To complete, press the paper flat, thereby making the bird's head and beak.

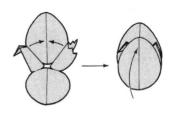

20 Repeat step 14. Press the paper flat.

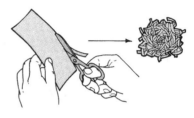

21 Cut a little of the rectangle, that you placed aside, into strips, so suggesting nesting material. Finally, write a message inside the card.

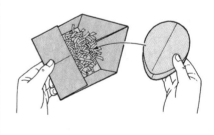

22 To send through the mail, place the nesting material and card into the envelope.

23 Open the card. The bird will pop-up.

MERRY CHRISTMAS

The following card looks very pretty when it is fixed on to a gift or displayed as a decoration.

You will need: *An 8½ x 11 in. sheet of white craft paper*
Scissors
Compass
Pencil
Felt-tip pen
Craft knife
A few colored sticky-backed circles and stars
Ribbon bow (see page 10)

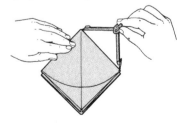

1 With the rectangle of white craft paper repeat steps 1 to 10 of the POP-UP BIRD (see page 22), but discarding the rectangle of paper in step 3.

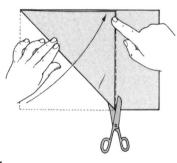

2 Using the compass, mark this quarter circle on to the preliminary base, as shown.

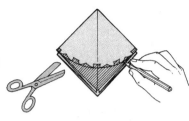

3 Using the pencil, mark out a fancy design around the quarter circle, as shown. Carefully cut around your pencil line and discard the shaded part.

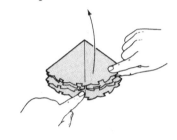

4 Open out the paper completely.

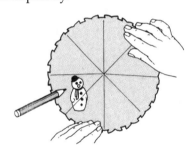

5 Using the felt-tip pen, draw this snowman design on to the paper's lower left-hand quarter, as shown. Place the upper half of the snowman's body (the part to be cut around in step 6) above the diagonal fold-line.

6 Carefully cut around the upper half of the snowman's body with the craft knife, as shown.

7 Decorate the card with the felt-tip pen, sticky-backed circles, stars and ribbon bow.

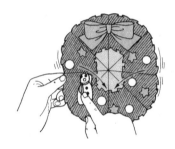

8 Put your finger on to the upper half of the snowman's body and push down, so that he is pushed through to the other side of the paper. While at the same time, re-folding the paper . . .

9 back to the beginning of step 4.

10 Finally, write a Christmas message on to the top layer of paper.

11 Open out the card completely for a perfect Christmas wreath.

Merry Christmas card

SNAPPING CROCODILE

If you want to make a special greeting card, where the receiver will have a surprise, then you will enjoy making this one.

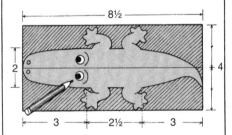

You will need:

Scissors
An 8½ x 11 in. sheet of craft paper
Ruler
Pencil
Felt-tip pen
Stick glue
A single card

1 Cut a rectangle measuring 4 x 8½ in. Using the pencil and ruler, mark and measure out this crocodile body design on to the rectangle, as shown. Using the felt-tip pen, draw on the crocodile's eyes. Carefully cut around your pencil lines and discard the shaded parts.

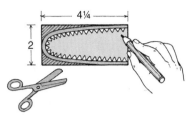

2 Cut a rectangle of craft paper measuring 2 x 4¼ in. Using the felt-tip pen, draw the crocodile's lower set of teeth on to the rectangle, as shown. Carefully cut around your pen lines and discard the shaded parts.

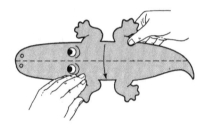

3 Place the crocodile's body sideways on. Fold it in half from top to bottom.

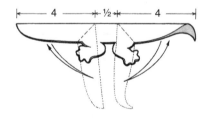

4 Fold the head and tail sections over, into the positions as shown by the measurements and dotted lines. Press the head and tail flat and unfold them.

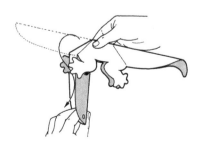

5 Inside reverse fold the head, along the fold-lines made in step 4 (see steps 16 to 19 of the POP-UP BIRD on page 23).

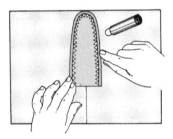

6 Repeat step 5 with the tail.

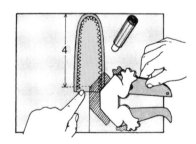

7 Open out the single card completely. Apply glue on to the back of the lower set of teeth and attach them on to the card, as shown.

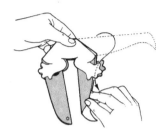

8 Turn the crocodile's body around, so that the folded edge points to the left. Apply glue on to the back of the body (not the head and tail) and attach it on to the card, as shown by the measurement and shaded part.

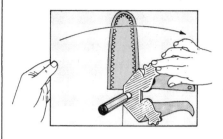

9 Apply glue on to the top of the body, as shown by the shaded part. Close the card in half from left to right and press firmly.

10 Make sure that the card opens and closes easily.

11 By opening and closing the card, the crocodile will snap its jaws and move its tail up and down. Finally, decorate the front of the card and write a message inside.

DO NOT FORGET

Like the previous card the receiver will have a surprise when they open it. Because inside there is an elephant!

You will need: *Scissors*
Ruler
An 8½ x 11 in. sheet of grey craft paper
Pencil
Felt-tip pen
A single card
Stick glue

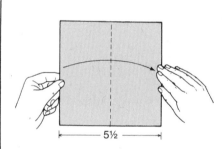

5½

1 Cut a 5½ in. square of grey craft paper. Fold it in half from left to right.

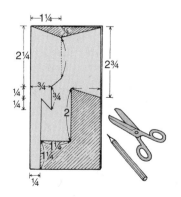

1¼
2¼
2¾
¼
¾
¾
¼
2
1¼
1¼
¼

2 Using the pencil and ruler, mark and measure out this elephant design on to the square, from the folded side, as shown. Carefully cut around your pencil lines and discard the shaded parts. Also cut along the solid line, as shown, so making the elephant's trunk and tusks.

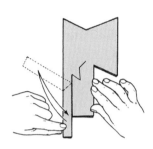

3 Fold the trunk over, into the position as shown by the dotted lines. Press the trunk flat and unfold it.

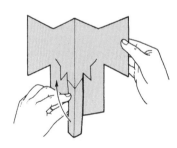

4 Fold the bottom layer of paper to the left, so making the elephant become three-dimensional. Do NOT press the paper flat. Lift the trunk up . . .

5 along the 'V' shaped fold-lines made in step 3.

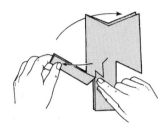

6 Fold the left-hand side behind to the right-hand side, so making the trunk stick out from the folded side. Press the paper flat.

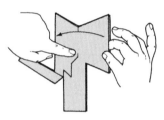

7 Fold the top layer of paper over, as shown by the dotted lines, while at the same time . . .

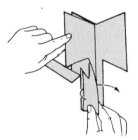

8 letting the top leg flick itself around.

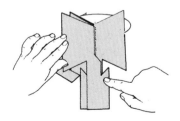

9 Repeat steps 7 and 8 on the bottom layer of paper.

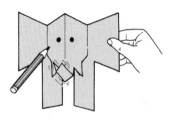

10 Open out the paper, so making the elephant become three-dimensional. Do NOT press the paper flat. Using the felt-tip pen, draw on the elephant's eyes.

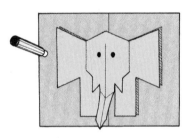

11 Open out the single card completely. Apply glue on to the back of the elephant's legs and ears (not the head, tusks and trunk), and attach them on to the card, as shown by the shaded parts.

12 Make sure that the card opens and closes easily.

13 By opening and closing the card, the elephant will move its trunk up and down. Finally, decorate the front of the card and write a message inside.

From the top: Do not forget;
Quacking duck; Snapping crocodile

QUACKING DUCK

Try experimenting with the following technique, and change the angle of the cut and folds, to see what other talking mouths you can design.

You will need: A double card
Pencil
Ruler
Scissors
An 8¼ x 11 in. rectangle of craft paper
Compass
Felt-tip pen

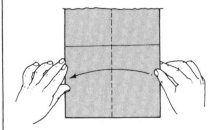

1 Open out the double card completely. Place the paper lengthways on. Fold it in half from right to left.

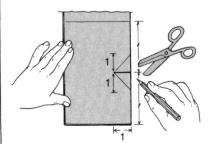

2 Put a pencil dot in the middle of the lower rectangle's folded side. Draw a 1 in. line from the dot towards the opposite side. Starting at the folded side, cut along the line.

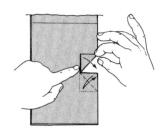

3 Fold the edges of the cut just made over, so making two triangles. Press the triangles flat and unfold them.

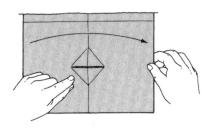

4 Open out the paper from left to right.

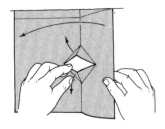

5 Pull the cut edges towards you, along the fold-lines made in step 3, while at the same time . . .

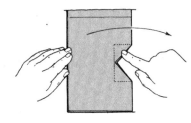

6 folding the paper in half from right to left, so forming a mouth-like shape inside. Press firmly and open.

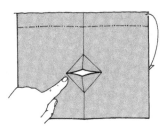

7 When you open and close the paper, the mouth will look as if it is talking. Fold the top edge behind to the bottom edge.

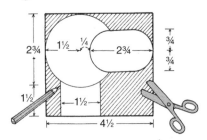

8 Cut a 4¼ x 4½ rectangle of craft paper. Using the compass, pencil and ruler, mark and measure out this duck design on to the rectangle, as shown. Carefully cut around your pencil lines and discard the shaded parts.

9 Using the felt-tip pen, draw on the duck's eye and a bow tie. Cut the beak in half, along the 2¾ pencil line marked in step 8.

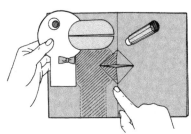

10 Apply glue on to the back of the duck and the part of the beak that is nearest the head. Attach the duck and its beak on to the card, as shown by the shaded part.

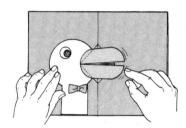

11 Should the duck's neck protrude pass the card's bottom edge, cut it off. Partly close the card, so folding the upper and lower parts of the beak along the dotted lines, as shown.

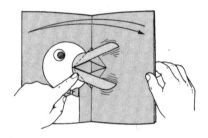

12 Make sure that the card opens and closes easily.

13 By opening and closing the card, the duck will appear to quack. Finally, decorate the front of the card and write a message inside.

MOTHERS' DAY

Paper flowers look most beautiful when they are arranged together. They also make ideal gifts to give on special occasions.

You will need: *A double card*
Pencil
Ruler
Scissors
Two different colored rectangles of gift wrapping paper
Stick glue

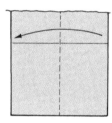

1 Open out the double card completely. Place the paper lengthways on. Fold it in half from right to left.

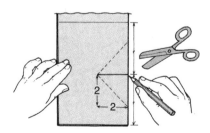

2 Put a pencil dot in the middle of the lower rectangle's folded side. Draw a 2 in. line from the dot towards the opposite side. Starting at the folded side, cut along the line.

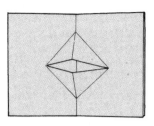

3 Repeat steps 3 to 7 of the QUACKING DUCK (see page 30).

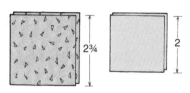

4 From one rectangle of gift wrapping paper cut two 2¾ in. squares, and from the other two 2 in. squares. Turn the squares around to look like diamonds, with their colored side on top. Fold them in half from top to bottom, making triangles. With each triangle repeat steps 4 to 10 of the POP-UP BIRD (see page 22).

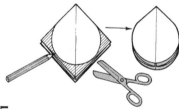

5 Using the pencil, mark out this petal design on to each of the bases, as shown. Carefully cut around your pencil lines and discard the shaded parts. You should now have two large flowers and two small ones.

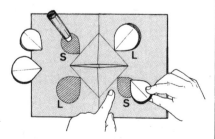

6 Apply glue on to the back of each flower and attach them on to the card, as shown by the indicated sizes and shaded parts.

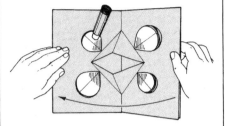

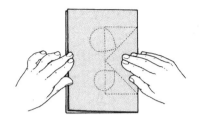

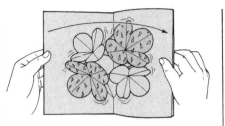

7 Apply glue on to the top of each flower, as shown by the shaded parts. Close the card in half from right to left and . . .

8 press firmly.

9 Make sure that the card opens and closes easily.

10 Open the card. The flowers will bloom. Finally, decorate the front of the card and write a message inside.

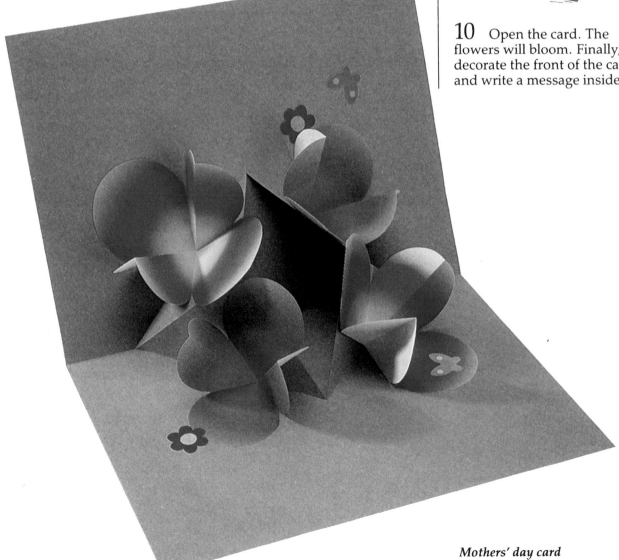

Mothers' day card

71160297R00044

Pulmonary Circulation
- - Answer - -

(1). Superior Vena Cava

(2). Pulmonary Artery

(3). Inferior Vena Cava

(4). Aorta

(5). Pulmonary Veins

(6). Heart

Pulmonary Circulation

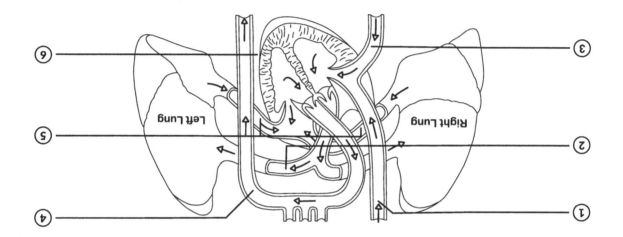

Right Lung

Left Lung

① ② ③ ④ ⑤ ⑥

Heart and Blood Circulation System

- - Answer - -

(1). Pulmonary Artery

(2). Right Atrium

(3). Right Ventricle

(4). Venae Cavae

(5). Capillaries

(6). Lungs

(7). Pulmonary Artery

(8). Left Atrium

(9). Left Ventricle

(10). Aorta

Heart and Blood Circulation System

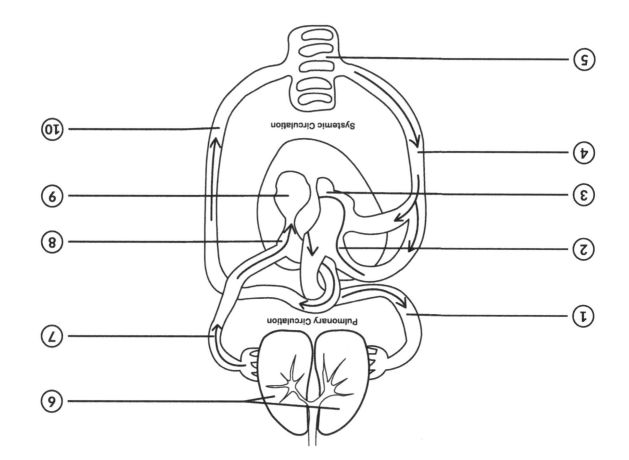

Systemic Circulation

Pulmonary Circulation

1
2
3
4
5
6
7
8
9
10

- - Answer - -

(1). Veins (From Body)

(2). Groove

(3). Artery (To Body)

(4). Artery (To Lungs)

(5). Veins (From Lungs)

(6). Apex

Heart-Ventral View

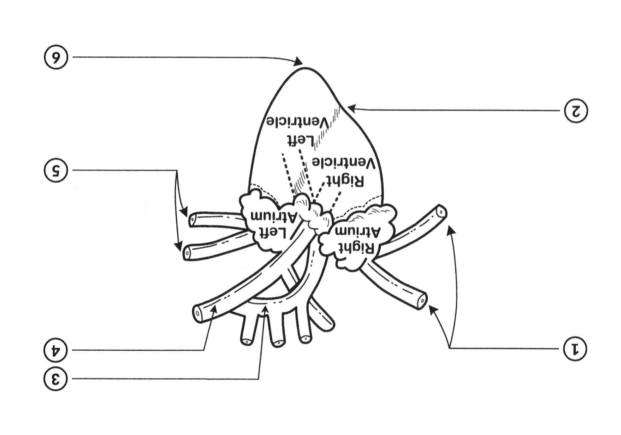

Right Ventricle

Left Ventricle

Left Atrium

Right Atrium